W9-CFB-174

EDGE BOOKS™

DRAW SCARY MONSTER MASH-UPS

BY Mari Bolte
ART BY Stefano Azzalin

CAPSTONE PRESS
a capstone imprint

Edge Books are published by Capstone Press,
1710 Roe Crest Drive, North Mankato, Minnesota 56003
www.mycapstone.com

Library of Congress Cataloging-in-Publication Data
Names: Bolte, Mari, author.
Title: Draw scary monster mash-ups / by Mari Bolte.
Description: North Mankato, Minnesota : Edge Books, Capstone Press,
2018. |
  Series: Drawing mash-ups | Includes bibliographical references and
index.
  | Audience: Ages 9-15. | Audience: Grades 4 to 6.
Identifiers: LCCN 2017021452 | ISBN 9781515769354 (library binding) |
ISBN 9781515769392 (ebook pdf)
Subjects: LCSH: Monsters in art--Juvenile literature. |
  Drawing—Technique—Juvenile literature.
Classification: LCC NC1764.8.M65 B65 2018 | DDC 741.5/37—dc23
LC record available at https://lccn.loc.gov/2017021452

Editorial Credits
Brann Garvey, designer; Kathy McColley, production specialist

Image Credits
Illustrations: Stefano Azzalin; Photos: Capstone Studio: Karon Dubke, 5
(all); Backgrounds and design elements: Capstone

Printed and bound in the USA.
010364F17

TABLE OF CONTENTS

SCARY SKETCHING

Does your creativity scare you? Get control of it through pen and paper! Smash two (or more!) unlikely combinations together to make a monstrous monster mash-up. Use the ideas in the book, and then re-mash them to make something even wilder! Challenge your friends to see who can draw the wildest monster combos.

MATERIALS

The artwork in this book was created digitally, but that doesn't mean your own art can't look equally amazing.

It all starts with a pencil and paper! Use light pencil strokes to shape your creation. Shading, hash marks, and curved lines can really make your mash-ups pop off the page.

When you're happy with how your sketches look, darken the pencil lines and erase any overlapping areas. Use a pen to outline and add shadows and detail.

Markers or colored pencils will truly bring your art to life. Experiment with shading, outlines, blending, or using different shades of the same color to make gradients. Or try out a new art supply! Chalk or watercolor pencils, oil crayons, or pastels could add an extra challenge.

BIG HAIR, BIG FEET

Here's a tip – find a stylist with great hair! This Sasquatch has long, lovely locks, and it can't wait to share its skills.

STEP 1

STEP 2

STEP 3

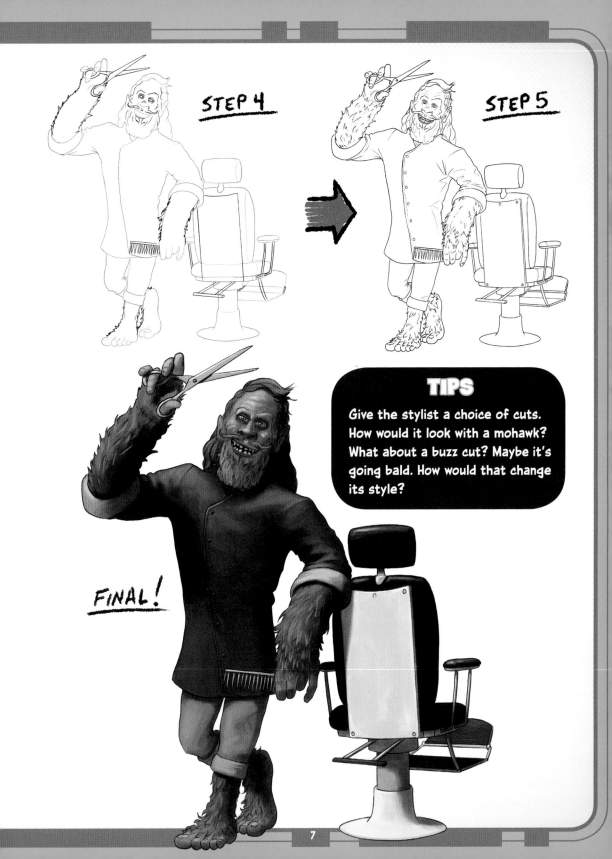

STEP 4

STEP 5

TIPS

Give the stylist a choice of cuts. How would it look with a mohawk? What about a buzz cut? Maybe it's going bald. How would that change its style?

FINAL!

UBER DEAD

Stick out your thumb and hail this cabbie from beyond the grave. He's a little hazy on directions, but you'll get from one place to another in the blink of an eye.

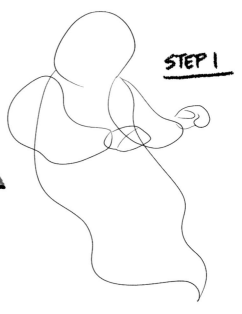

STEP 1

STEP 2

STEP 3

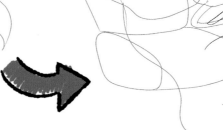

STEP 4

STEP 5

FINAL!

TIPS

What kind of car does this cabbie drive? Take the next step and sketch out his supernatural ride.

TECH TERROR

There's no use restarting your devices when this gremlin is around. Worse than a virus, he'll make sure your high-tech gadgets crash every time.

STEP 1

STEP 2

STEP 3

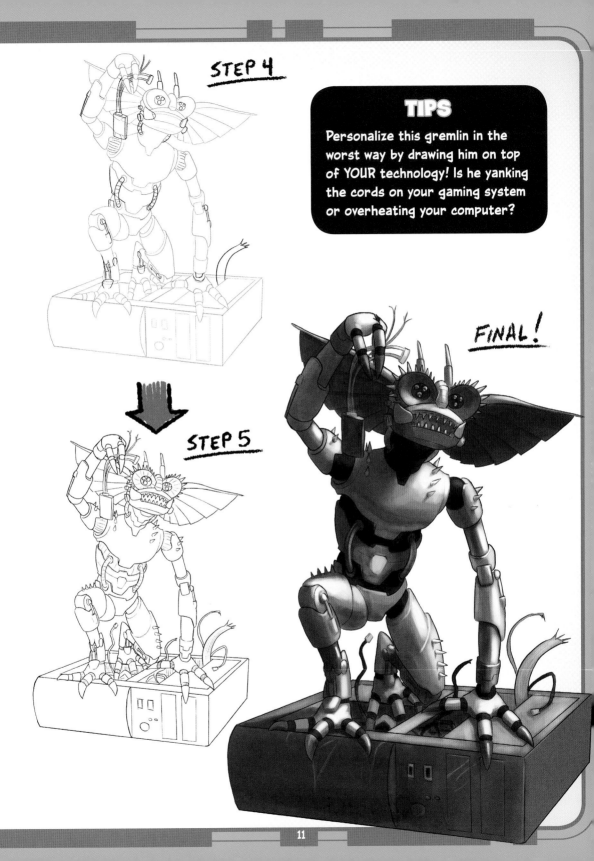

STEP 4

TIPS

Personalize this gremlin in the worst way by drawing him on top of YOUR technology! Is he yanking the cords on your gaming system or overheating your computer?

STEP 5

FINAL!

LAB LIZARD

Lab rats are overrated. Lab lizards are the mad scientists of the future! Get ready to take over the world with one of the extreme experiments this lizard will let loose.

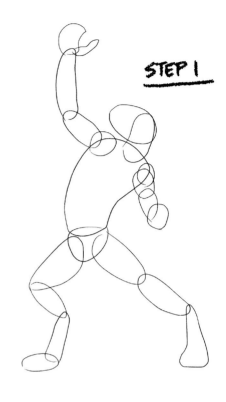

STEP 1

STEP 2

STEP 3

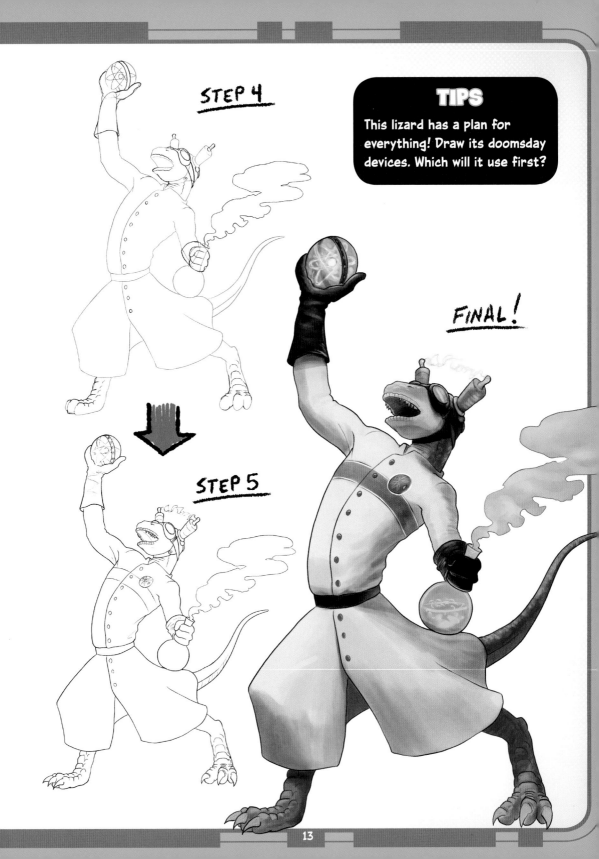

STEP 4

TIPS

This lizard has a plan for everything! Draw its doomsday devices. Which will it use first?

FINAL!

STEP 5

CHEF WASABI

Release the kraken – in the kitchen! Make maki, sashimi, nigiri, and any other types of sushi you can imagine. They'll come to life under this squid chef's tentacles.

STEP 1

STEP 2

STEP 3

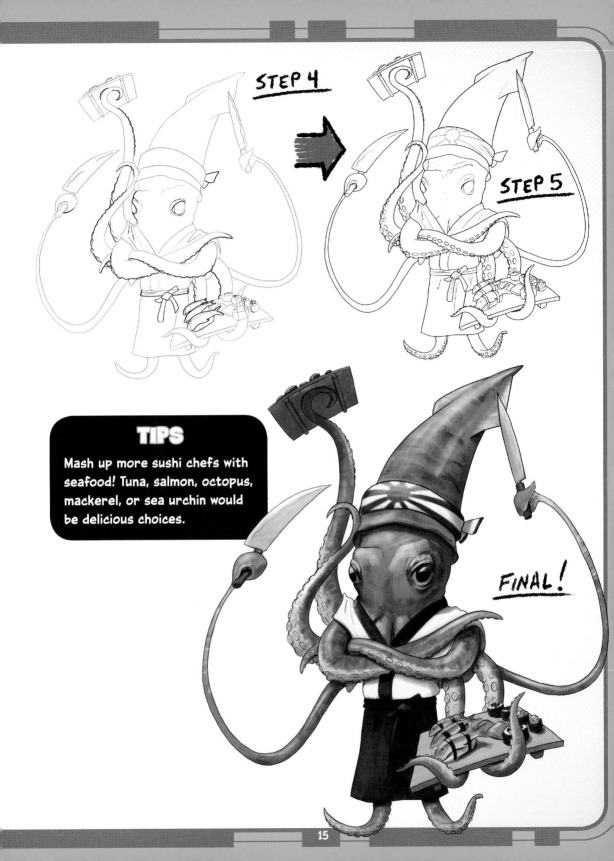

STEP 4

STEP 5

TIPS

Mash up more sushi chefs with seafood! Tuna, salmon, octopus, mackerel, or sea urchin would be delicious choices.

FINAL!

SHARK-O-SAURUS REX

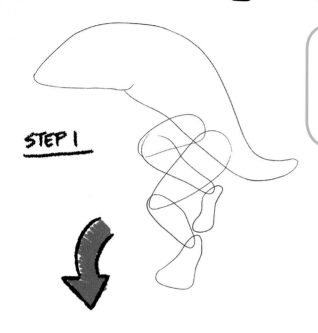

Run – and swim – for your life! No one is safe on land or sea while this shark-o-saurus rex is on the hunt.

STEP 1

STEP 2

STEP 3

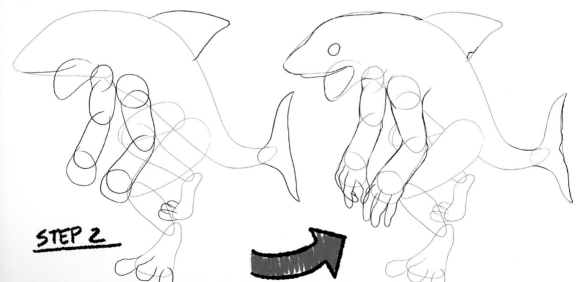

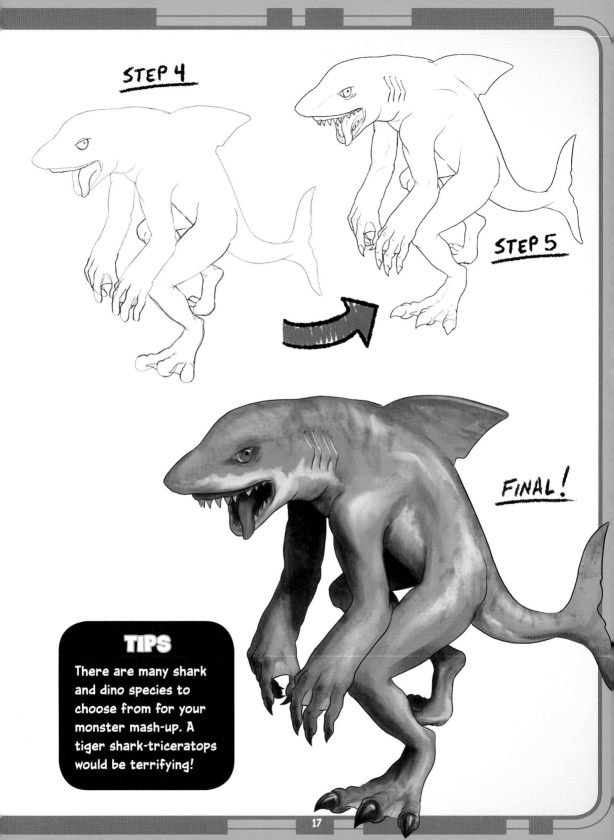

STEP 4

STEP 5

FINAL!

TIPS

There are many shark and dino species to choose from for your monster mash-up. A tiger shark-triceratops would be terrifying!

HOWLING AT THE MOON CAKES

Fresh-baked bread is a perk when your baker is up early to howl at the moon. Get there at the crack of dawn for the best breakfast ever. (Just don't wear your red cape!)

STEP 1

STEP 2

STEP 3

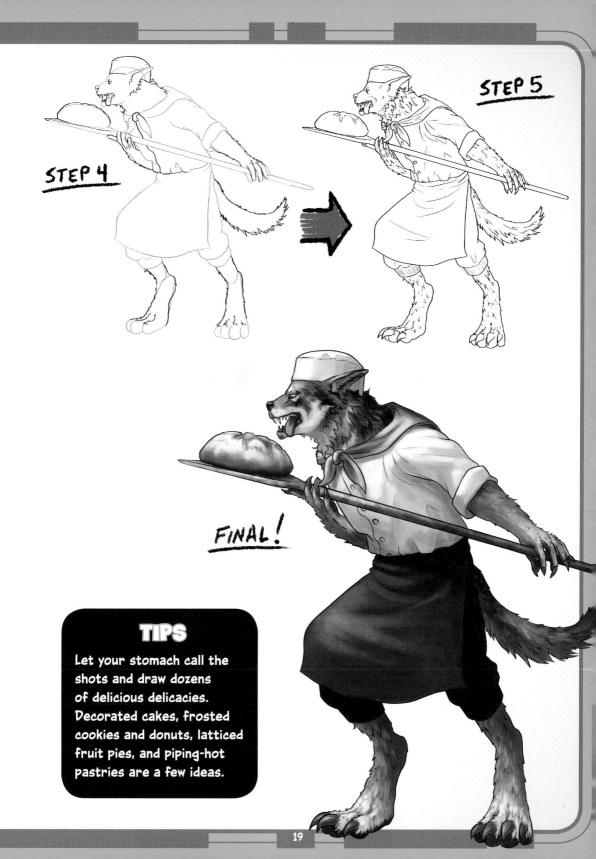

STEP 4

STEP 5

FINAL!

TIPS

Let your stomach call the shots and draw dozens of delicious delicacies. Decorated cakes, frosted cookies and donuts, latticed fruit pies, and piping-hot pastries are a few ideas.

DOCTOR Z, PHD

Bad news – this doctor doesn't have the cure to anything. (Hint: Most doctors don't advise biting as an appropriate form of medical care!)

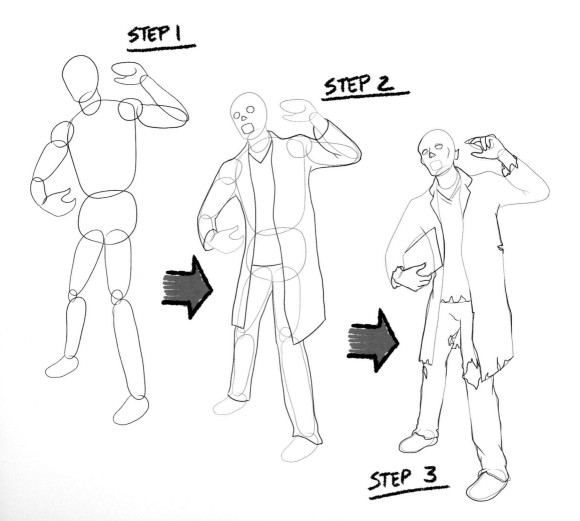

STEP 1

STEP 2

STEP 3

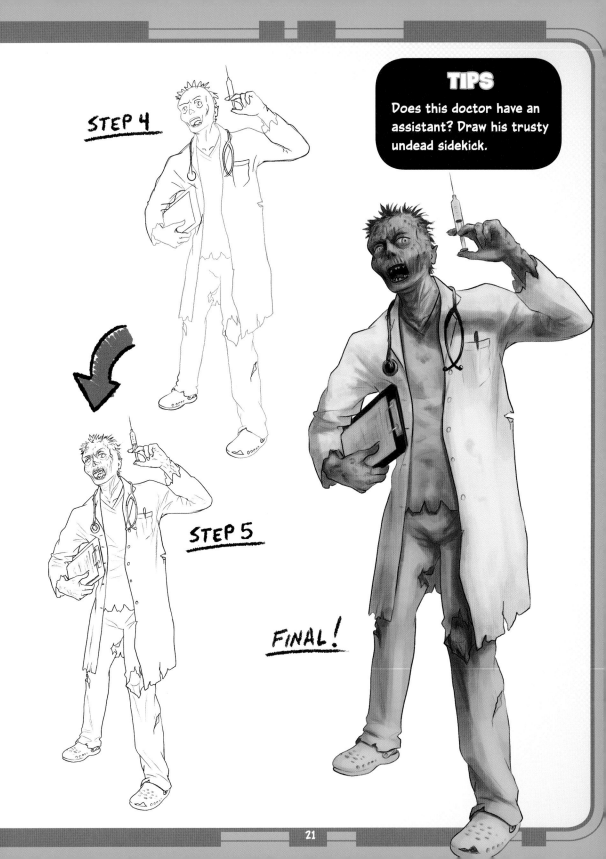

STEP 4

TIPS

Does this doctor have an assistant? Draw his trusty undead sidekick.

STEP 5

FINAL!

MACHO MINOTAUR

Potholes are a danger for both wheels and hooves. But there's no need to worry when this bullheaded construction worker is on duty.

STEP 1

STEP 2

STEP 3

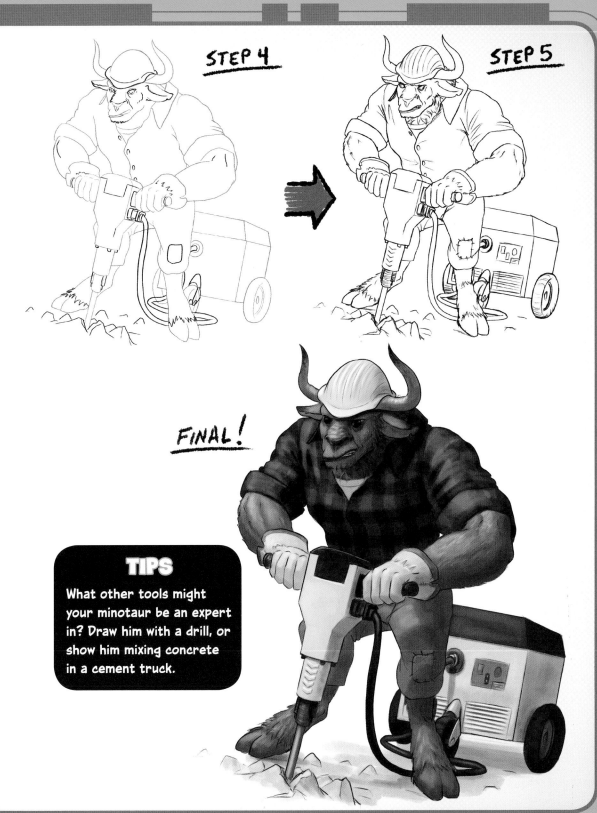

STEP 4

STEP 5

FINAL!

TIPS

What other tools might your minotaur be an expert in? Draw him with a drill, or show him mixing concrete in a cement truck.

FRANKENSTEIN'S MEGA MONSTER

Frankenstein's monster fighting evil as a spandex-wearing superhero? You'd better believe it! He runs on electricity, so there's a never-ending supply of power.

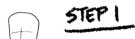

STEP 1

STEP 2

STEP 3

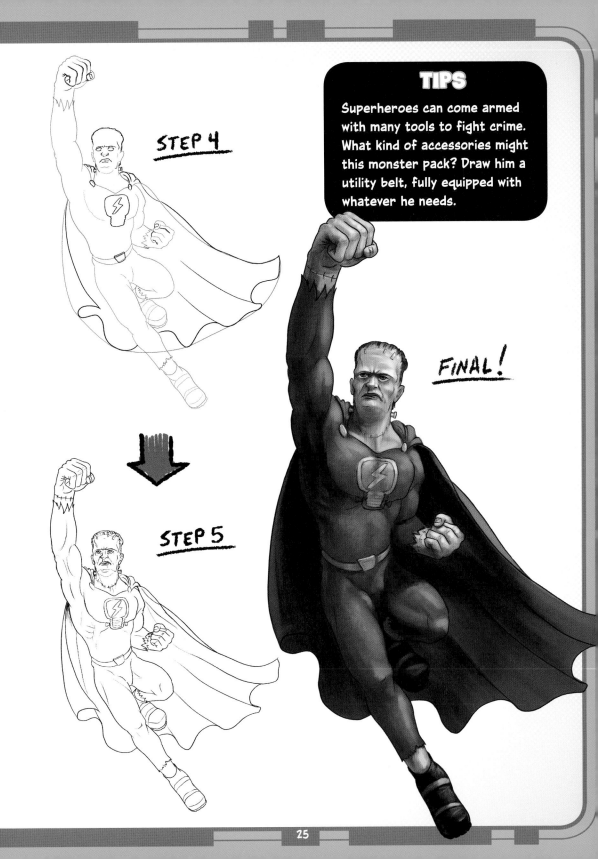

STEP 4

TIPS

Superheroes can come armed with many tools to fight crime. What kind of accessories might this monster pack? Draw him a utility belt, fully equipped with whatever he needs.

FINAL!

STEP 5

PHARAOH'S POLICE

Pharaoh can rest in peace for eternity knowing he's being watched over. Tomb robbers will think twice before committing a crime when this cursed cop is on patrol.

STEP 1

STEP 2

STEP 3

STEP 4

STEP 5

FINAL!

POLICE

TIPS

Get inspired by ancient Egyptian art and culture to create the coolest cop cycle. Sphinxes, cheetahs, and ibis would make the undead-mobile amazing.

FEARSOME FANGS

Tigers like to stick to the shadows — and so do vampires! They're a natural monster mash-up.

STEP 1

STEP 2

STEP 3

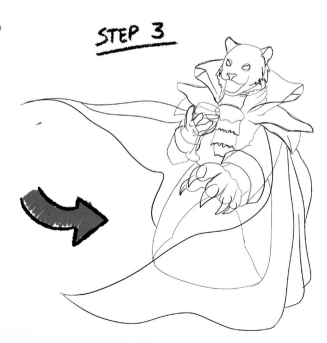

STEP 4

STEP 5

FINAL!

TIPS

For extra spook, mash up the bats, too. How horrified would you be if a tiger-headed bat flew at your face?

THE CLOWN UNDER THE BRIDGE

As if trolls weren't spooky enough! This clown troll is the stuff of nightmares.

STEP 1

STEP 2

STEP 3

STEP 4

FINAL!

STEP 5

READ MORE

Bird, Benjamin. *Monster Doodles With Scooby-Doo!* North Mankato, Minn.: Capstone Press, 2017.

Gowen, Fiona. *How to Draw Scary Monsters and Other Mythical Creatures.* Hauppauge, N.Y.: Barrons Educational Series, Inc., 2017.

Young, Tim. *Creatures and Characters: Drawing Amazing Monsters, Aliens, and Other Weird Things!* Atglen, Penn.: Schiffer Pub., Ltd., 2017.

INTERNET SITES

Use FactHound to find Internet sites related to this book.

Visit *www.facthound.com*

Just type in 9781515769354 and go.

 Check out projects, games and lots more at
www.capstonekids.com